to Live
and
to Conquer

a memoir by
Kaitlyn Harmon

TREATY OAK PUBLISHERS

PUBLISHER'S NOTE

This is a work of personal memoir and inspiration. All of the characters, business establishments, and events are based on the author's personal experiences. Individuals' names may have been changed to protect their privacy.

Printed and published in the United States of America

TREATY OAK PUBLISHERS

ISBN-13: 978-1-943658-31-2

Available in print and digital from Amazon

DEDICATION

To my parents.
Thank you for being my heroes,
my people, and my light.

NOTE FROM THE AUTHOR

I hope this book serves as a helping hand, a shoulder to cry on, an ear that listens. I hope you know that you're not alone in this great big world and that whatever comes your way in life, you can handle.

Yet, more importantly, I hope this book rekindles your fire and shows you your strength, importance, worth, and beauty. May your path be a path worth traveling and your life a life worth living.

TABLE OF CONTENTS

to Live

and

to Conquer

INTRODUCTION

For such a long time I felt not normal. Unwanted. Not good enough. Not pretty enough. Not fast enough. Not enough. But then at some point in this complex, messy thing we call life, the negativity and insecurities seemed to vanish. And then there I was, dancing it out, standing in the sun, and being my own person.

Chapter 1
THE START

From the very first breath I took, I was different. Still different to this very day. I think differently, act differently, respond differently. But I no longer think being different is a bad thing.

I worship it. I take it all in and praise the heavens above because I was made to be different, just like every other human being on this Earth. Different in beautiful, unique ways.

Never have I been a social butterfly; in fact, the thought of being in a group of people scares me to death. It suffocates me, takes over my mind, makes me feel uncomfortable and squeamish. Makes me want to disappear by magic and time travel back to my house, back to when I was younger, back to a peaceful state of mind.

One day, all of my nervousness and discomfort skyrocketed at what seemed like a hundred thousand miles per hour, and then I hit my low point. I stopped going to school, stopped exercising, stopped talking to friends, stopped interacting with people. Stopped everything. I was no longer this sweet girl most people thought I was.

Even during this period of my life when I was down in the trenches, people still thought of me as a sweet and intelligent person because the pain—my pain—blinded them. I learned to hide my deepest, darkest emotions. I smiled, laughed, conversed with people, but without meaning all of those things. I was just faking it. Faking it till I made it.

I lost my love of life. I stopped thinking of the world as a happy place because it became this dark, sad, tragic planet I was forced to call home, be a part of, and live my life daily. In truth, I had nowhere else to go. Much as I would have loved it, I couldn't hop on a space shuttle and fly off into the galaxy.

Stuck here, I dug a hole for myself down into the deep, never-ending trench, down to the core of the Earth, and no one and nothing could pull me back up. As much love and support as I had and still do have, there were—and still are—times when I feel like it's just me, taking on this great big world, having to drag myself up unaccompanied. I didn't even feel like God spoke to me, supported me, or encouraged me.

I felt completely and utterly alone. Lonely as lonely gets.

> I was no longer this sweet girl most people thought I was.

Therapy, medication, new environments, new coping mechanisms - nothing worked. I felt damaged, mentally and physically. I no longer wanted to fight to have friends. I wanted to sleep all the time, to curl up in my bedroom with a blanket and my laptop and binge watch shows on Netflix because I couldn't bear the thought of being in my world for another second. I wanted out, and if that meant watching a handful of shows numerous times, then that's what it was going to take.

I was desperate.

And then something miraculous happened. I became reaffirmed in my faith because I was afraid of being alone. But I wouldn't be alone if He were with me, so I began to trust in God again, or at least the idea of Him.

When we hit the lowest of low points, we turn to whatever and to whomever we can rely on. It's a time of desperateness and despair, a time when we turn to anything just to hold on longer because we have no other choice. I prayed because I had nothing left to turn to. My community had diminished and all I had left was God. I started to pray one night and one simple conversation with God is what led me home. He guided me back home.

Prayers came to me and I could feel and see my prayers being answered. I fell in love with life again. I wanted to fight for the wellbeing of me. I wanted to be strong. I wanted to be that sweet, intelligent, caring girl who was happy on both the inside and the outside. A girl who no longer needed to fake it to get by.

I fell in love with me, and I did that through finding my passion. I found my spark, my fire, my determination. I saw who I was and who I wanted to become. I was a broken teenager who wanted to be a new type of different. I also saw the skinny, fearful, dependent girl who could become a strong, fearless, independent woman.

At the time, I may not have seen these exact things, but I knew I wanted to put my mind, spirit, and body into something. And I'm so glad I did. I'm so proud that I dug myself out of that deep, deep trench. I'm proud I was at last able to accept and recognize that something was wrong with me, something I didn't like or appreciate. And I'm so glad I said a prayer and wished at 11:11 PM countless nights that something would change.

Believe you can and you're halfway there.

-Theodore Roosevelt

Chapter 2
ACCEPTING YOURSELF

If I've learned anything along this complex, messy, happy, joyful journey, it's that I need to love myself. I need to love my insecurities, my flaws, my personality, my appearance. I need to love me for me.

At the end of the day, with maybe no one you can lean on or talk to, you've got to lean on yourself. You've got to say, "Let's do this, girl."

You've got to tell yourself, this isn't going to be easy one bit, but if you're serious, you can put your mind to anything and accomplish it. If you want to run a six-minute mile, do it. If you want to be a better Christian, do it. If you want to love others more, do it.

Because there's absolutely nothing you can't do or be. Don't listen to the people who tell you something is wrong with you, that you can't be this or that, that you can't do this or that. Because, you know what? They're flat out wrong. No one knows you better than you, and only you know you can do whatever you set your mind to, conquer your mind.

I told myself I could and I did.

Stop procrastinating, stop saying you can't. Do it. Do it, girl... seriously. I believe in you. I'm here to tell you that you can do whatever you put your mind to because I'm proof.

I wouldn't be writing this if I hadn't believed I could change. I wouldn't be writing this if I didn't want to support you in any way possible.

So many people have told me things get better, the light is near, all my worries and fears will vanish because God is here, He is present. And for a while, I didn't believe one word. I would nod my head and say, "I know," while my eyes flooded with tears. Not because people said everything would end soon, that this pain would go away. I cried because I didn't believe it. Because I've experienced so much pain and so much false hope that I had nothing else to believe.

And, let me tell you, I was so wrong. Those people were right.

That light at the end of the tunnel was so near at the time that it blinded me. Like I was drowning in a swimming pool, and above me I saw this blob of light that was so bright, that I had to close my eyes. I wasn't able to open them because I was in so much pain. I was done. Done.

And yet, I held on. I decided to put all my might and energy into action and swim to where the sand meets the tides, and get up and out of the water. And I did it. I told myself I could and I did.

And the most amazing thing is that I didn't need anyone to tell me to swim to land and get out of the water. I didn't need anyone to tell me to hold on. I told myself.

There's this feeling you get when you accomplish something you didn't think you could do. The feeling of running over five miles and feeling so happy and proud of yourself that you didn't throw up or faint. You kept on running, you picked up the pace, and you pulled through.

Not for anyone, but for yourself.

To love someone else, you have to love yourself first. I promise it's not selfish… You have to first have faith in yourself and all you're capable of. You have to accept you for you. You have to be your own person and be proud of it.

The definition of loving yourself takes many forms, and out of all those definitions, there's one thing in common: *Accept you for you.* You cannot love someone else with your whole heart or care for that person unless you love yourself, and to love yourself you have to grasp the basic: accept yourself.

And then "treat yo self," if you know what I mean.

*When I accept myself, I am freed from
the burden of needing you to accept me.*

-Dr. Steve Maraboli

Chapter 3
RECOGNIZING THE PAIN

The first step to solving a problem is identifying it. I was fortunate enough to have people in my life who could recognize my problem—my pain—before I could. They may not have understood it, but they saw it and accepted the fact that something needed to be done; something needed to change or something needed to happen.

Of course, when you're a kid, your parents are the ones who are supposed to look after you. To care of you. To love on you when you need loving, or to harp on you when you need harping.

My parents did all of those things, plus more. They recognized my unhappiness before I could. They saw me moping around the house, sleeping whenever I got the chance to sleep, stepping back from my daily activities of homework, volleyball, and friends. They went—and still do—go above and beyond to ensure I'm happy and healthy.

I was fading and falling quickly, and thank God they were there to catch me.

Now, you're probably wondering, *How do I recognize the pain?*

Simply ask yourself if you're happy. Maybe you log your daily actions or conversations. Create a list of things that are on your mind: are they more negative or positive? Keep a running log of things you're interested in, or things you want to be, and if you're not that, then you've found the problem.

I didn't do all of these things myself. I was told to, but I didn't. You know how life is just one huge experiment—trial and error? I never had a starting point. Things just happened over time, and my mindset changed. That's how I reset my path, and I still continue to do so each day. I fully put my life, worries, dreams, and ambitions in the hands of the universe, in the hands of God, and for the first time in my life, I realized that I couldn't control everything. And from there, things got a little bit easier day by day, week by week, as I was finally able to live my life without fear and worry. I was free.

Do whatever works for you. I kept a mental log of things I wanted to see in myself, things I was interested in, and things that I thought and said throughout the day. And very slowly I found that I truly wasn't happy, that my parents were right.

> Do
> whatever works
> for you.

It may or may not take you a long time to identify the problem and eventually the pain, but you'll find it if it's there. After all, pain is inevitable, but yours doesn't have to be permanent.

Find a person: a friend, a parent, a mentor, a doctor, anyone. Talk to them. Tell them how you're feeling.

One of the many things I've learned is that it's beyond helpful to talk to someone, anyone. It may take trial and error to find someone who understands, or maybe doesn't understand, but wants to be that shoulder for you to lean on. It'll all work out in time, I promise.

The power to change your life is in your hands.
The journey is yours.
Make today the day you take charge.

-Elle Sommer

Chapter 4
FINDING THE SPARK

I needed courage to get out of bed on the days that are the hardest. I call them the "blah days." In the past, I've seemed to have a lot of them, and I still do. Everyone does because we're human.

But there will come a day where the blah days end, and you know why? Because you've found a special thing called "the spark."

I found my spark on a blah day. I can't remember what exactly happened, or what I was doing, but what I can remember is that a switch flipped and my mind, my mentality, my attitude changed.

That spark for me was fitness. People who know me also know I have a passion for sports, so naturally I'm an athletic person, an athlete. Finding that switch wasn't quite that difficult, but what was difficult was getting out of the funk I was living in.

It takes time to develop a habit. So, I had to get out of bed each day for a period of time, where I flipped the switch, and eventually that switch stayed flipped for good.

Finding the spark means doing something that makes you happy.

Finding the spark means doing something that makes you happy. Something you enjoy and would do regardless if someone or something disapproved. Some people made fun of me for exercising with so much passion, for working out every single day one summer. For becoming a health nut, even though, let's face it, I've always been a health nut.

But I didn't care. Yes, maybe those comments might have stung a little, I cannot deny that, but I kept doing what made me happy: exercising. Working out is my stress reliever, my therapy, my home away from home that doesn't really exist, because working out isn't a place, but you get the point.

It's like working out had become my new best friend, and it was, without a doubt, the one thing I needed to turn my life around.

Now, when I say these things in my life really have turned my life around, I mean it. I may not be the person who made the smartest decisions in the world, but then someone came along and told me to clean up my mess and get my act together. That person was me.

The people I had in my life and still do today (because, let's face it, you need to keep those people around), were the ones who helped me turn my life around. If it weren't for them, I don't even know what my life would look like right now. It's unfathomable.

I'm not claiming I would be a druggie who makes poor choices; I just probably would not have been as mature and stable as I needed to be. I would have been isolated and reclusive. I wouldn't have had friends or a social life, I would have been confined to my bedroom, binge-watching shows, as I tried to escape this thing called my life. Simply put, I would be emotionally empty and weak: inept.

The spark equals passion. Your passions.

Take time to think, please pause right now, and just process and think about your passions. Not your friend's passions or the trendy passions, your passions.

I know my fabulous writing is going to be hard to put down, but stop reading, I beg you.

The point is, finding the spark takes time, establishing the spark takes time, but it's all worth it. My advice to you, if you're still reading this, is to do what makes you happy. It's a lot easier said than done, but doing it— finding the spark, the happiness—is worth the pain, the confusion, and the unhappiness that you were, are, or will be going through at some point in your life.

Passion is energy.
Feel the power that comes from focusing
on what excites you.

-Oprah Winfrey

Chapter 5
LIVING LIFE TO THE FULLEST

The phrase "living life to the fullest" makes me want to vomit, or at least it used to have that effect on me. The number of people who have told me to do this, to branch out, to go out of my comfort zone, to leave the bubble, is ridiculous. But what they said to encourage me was and is so true. I'm embarrassed even admitting this, but you do only live once, truly... What the heck, I'm going to yolo for the heck of it, yolo.

I'd say the second I branched out, the instant I ventured out of my comfort zone was such a basic, odd moment, but I did it. If you're dying to know about it, my story is for you.

It was freshman year homecoming. Homecoming. I'm disgusted I'm even telling this story.

I stood in the middle of the gym with some friends, and a song came on the speaker, one we all loved. People started dancing. In truth, I am not a dancer in the slightest bit; in fact, I don't think I've ever danced in my life. If you had seen me at cotillion, you would have noticed I was the awkward girl standing way too close to a guy while everyone else danced.

Laugh, cry, and smile.

Now, back to the story. Oh yes, everyone started dancing, or as I like to think of it, just jumping up and down, sweating in a pit of people. As my friends told me to dance, all I could think was that I wanted to go home, that I showed up at this dance, which should have been enough, that I had fulfilled my commitment for the night, but thanks to my friends at the time, I danced. I mean

I jumped up and down, but it's the same thing, right?

I know this sounds so stupid and odd, so not normal, but for me, this was the moment when I went out of my comfort zone. To be honest, I believe we're all born out of our comfort zones. I can't exactly put it into words why, but I think we just are.

I don't live my life to the fullest every day, every month, or every year, but I do try. On my journey of "resuscitating" my life, I've learned that we all really do live once, so we need to live our lives to the fullest: cherish time with your family, your friends, your God. Laugh, cry, and smile. Experience all the aspects of life: the good, the bad, the hideous. At the end of the day, as long as you're experiencing life, then you're living it to the fullest, even if you're not backpacking through Europe, climbing Mount Everest, or visiting every single country of the continental world.

To live is the rarest thing in the world.
Most people just exist.

-Oscar Wilde

Chapter 6
LA VIE EST BELLE

On random occasions, I wear three bangles, and frankly, I should wear them more often. They're called *mantra* bracelets.

I've always been a fan of quotes and #MantraMondays, so having non-permanent reminders on my wrist seems appropriate. But between you and me, I hope to one day make those reminders permanent, if you know what I mean... Keep it on the DL.

But two of these bracelets make me think. One, because they're in other languages. And, two, because they can be perceived multiple ways.

"La vie est belle" is French for "life is beautiful." Seeing this mantra makes me think about a couple of different things, one being the meaning of life in general. How life only comes around one time, we only get one shot, and I should cherish it as much as I can.

The second thing it makes me think about is the actual anatomy of life. Being an anatomy nerd, I can admit the complexity of the human body astounds me. How the heart's intricate and delicate design lets it pump blood throughout your entire body, and how the brain creates your most vivid thoughts and emotions.

> I appreciate life a little more.

Both are beyond me, but considering these two simple yet complex things amazes me. I appreciate life a little more. The lone reason I want to be a surgeon is because of how interesting and breathtaking the human body is. It's nothing short of astonishing.

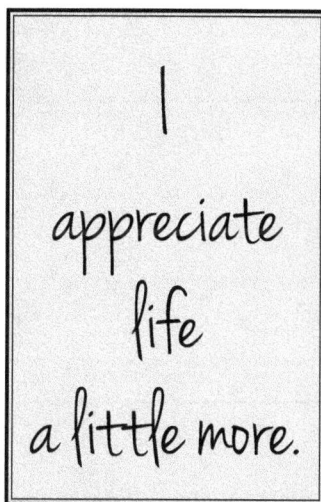

So, yes, life is beautiful because God specifically made it 7.4 billion plus times. As sad or happy as it may be, the ending of a life and the beginning of one within a few seconds is jaw-dropping.

When my brother was born, I discovered that life truly is magnificent. The day he was born, my life changed. One day, our house was chaotic and stressful, and the next was at complete peace. It's like God hand-delivered a miracle, if you will, to our doorstep.

The idea of this tiny little alien-like thing who was nurtured in the same womb I was nurtured in, and then I'm holding this thing in my very arms, is more than extraordinary. Not to get too sentimental, but wow. I almost can't wrap my mind around it.

The two meanings of "la vie est belle" coincide with each other because at the end of the day God made life, a billion times, probably even more, and we were all put on this very soil, holy soil we all have a hand in, because God wanted to share His beauty and love, His masterpiece with all of us.

*Life is beautiful, and
there's so much to smile about.*

-Marilyn Monroe

Chapter 7
ALIS VOLAT PROPRIIS

"She flies with her own wings."

It's Latin.

Of all of the letters in the English alphabet, and the countless combinations we can make with them, this one is by far my favorite.

I've always been a fan of the independent. I root for the girl who's ambitious in her actions and in her voice. The girl who roars at the top of her lungs because she is not afraid to be heard. The girl who doesn't need a guy in her life to make her feel prettier, stronger, or even smarter. The girl who can build her own desk and fix her own car.

I'm that girl. I'm the independent. Except... I can't fix a car. Not yet.

In the past year, so many people have revealed themselves to be opposed to individuality and women. And to be honest, I don't understand why. Someone, please tell me what is so wrong with any type of woman being an individual and going after life, just tackling it head on.

To me, *alis volat propriis* means shattering glass ceilings, using your voice, and defying the odds. It means ignoring all the shit people think about and call you by. It means not being afraid to embrace yourself and this messed up world we live in. It means going into a sea of seven thousand people who disagree with every single word that comes out of your mouth and remaining firm in your beliefs.

Be your own person and fly with your own wings. You have nothing to lose in this life. And even if you did have something to forfeit, why not lose while fighting in the pursuit for what you believe in? Nothing is more courageous and victorious than fighting the good fight. Because it means you've already won. You're the victor.

We live in a preconceived world where men have always dominated everything. Now, I am not claiming that women have not come a long way, because we have and it's remarkable.

However, this world is dominated by men, and many people still believe men are morally superior to women. If this is your opinion, then I respect you and your beliefs because we are all entitled to think, feel, and speak whatever we want, but I have to say that I disagree with you, if you can't already tell.

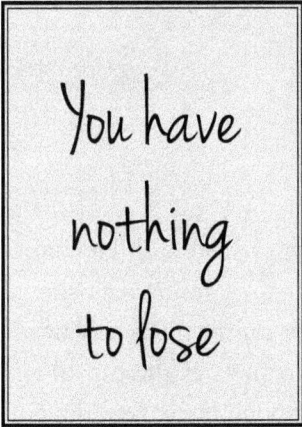

As a young woman, I believe women have the opportunity to shatter the glass ceiling so many times that there are no more ceilings remaining to be shattered. I'm an optimist and I believe the time for women is now. I believe that a woman flying with her own wings, in her own identity, in her own personality, in her own style, is courageous and awe-inspiring.

You have nothing to lose

I believe anyone—whether you're male or female or transgender, homosexual or heterosexual, republican or democrat, black or white—should be respected. Nothing is more courageous, bold, or amazing than standing up and being you, all of you to the fullest extent and embracing it.

Be you, girl. Fly with your own damn wings. You do not need anyone to help you fly because you are strong as hell.

So wear your strongest posture now,
and see your hardest times as
more than
just the time you fell
but a range of mountains
you learned to climb.

-Morgan Harper Nichols

Chapter 8
You Are Important

If you're on this earth, you're important. Your worth is immeasurable and unmatchable. In every person's life, a time comes when they wish they weren't alive.

At least that's my dark, twisted perception. It's happened to me, and I won't shy away from the subject. I often wondered if my absence on this earth would cause anyone pain, and for a while I believed it wouldn't because I wasn't deemed important. I didn't deem myself important.

I was wrong. Some person in this world cares about you in such an intricate way that your absence would cause them an unfathomable pain. You are important and please never think otherwise.

You were put on this earth for a reason. Whether that reason is to meet someone, change someone's life, change lives, cure cancer, stop an atomic bomb, you are important.

Let me say that again. *You are important.*

What makes someone important is not their physical appearance or their popularity. No, what makes someone important is the amount of love in their heart. With all my heart, mind, and soul I believe the difference between someone who loves and someone who hates comes down to one simple characteristic: confidence.

Having confidence in yourself means you realize how important you

> You are important simply because you exist

are and how big an asset you are to humankind. A person who loves is someone who knows their worth is immeasurable because they're making a difference. They're making a difference in the world by giving some piece of themselves away, by submerging some piece of themselves into the air, and doing it with love, passion, and confidence.

A person who hates is someone who does not know their own worth. I would go as far to say that people who hate think life is a game: you lose some and you win some, and you'll do anything to win, even if that means destroying everything and everyone in your path.

Simply put, you are important because you matter to someone. You are important to whatever you believe in: God, Buddha, Nirvana. You are important simply because you exist.

If only you could sense
how important you are to
the lives of those you meet;
how important you can be
to people you may never even dream of.
There is something of yourself that
you leave at every meeting
with another person.

-Fred Rogers

Chapter 9
YOU ARE BEAUTIFUL

Christina Aguilera's song makes a sensational entrance into my head when I read the title of this chapter. You know that song that goes, "I am beautiful no matter what they say, words can't bring me down?" Yes, that one. Those lyrics speak for themselves.

Every single person is beautiful in their own unique way; beautiful regardless of skin color, race, gender, religion. Every single person is beautiful because every single person is one in countless millions. We all bring an unmatched beauty to the table simply by being ourselves and being who we are at our core: different. Your uniqueness makes you beautiful.

We often believe our beauty is a measure of the lusciousness of our hair, the absence of acne on our skin, and the skinniness of our waists. *It isn't.*

At the end of the day, no one truly cares if you are pretty or even attractive. If anything, good looks can get you to very minimal places in life, but a beautiful charisma is what matters most and is what can help you reach your maximum potential.

So you don't resemble one of the women on *People Magazine's* 'World's Most Beautiful.' So what? Being a size 0 or a size 12 cannot measure your beauty. You are beautiful in your own way. Each body shape is exquisite because you were created in the image of your Creator. You were meant to wear a certain body shape and own it. Own your uniqueness and own that body you were blessed with!

While beauty is measured by uniqueness and not by skinniness, the absence of acne, or the lusciousness of hair, and while I do agree with everything I have preached, I also want to emphasize the following: there's a difference between beauty and true beauty.

Beauty is simply having a beautiful personality, but true beauty is having a beautiful heart and soul that hopes in the darkest of times and loves in the cruelest of times. True beauty is the ability to be confident, to know your worth, to live life to the fullest, and be the true you. In short, genuine beauty is just doing you and being you every waking minute of every day.

There's a difference between beauty and true beauty.

And if I were on some TV show right now and heard someone say that, then I would say, "That shit is beautiful." And it really is.

Your beauty is measured by how you view yourself: *unique*. Beauty comes from within. Always look in the mirror and know you're beautiful. And if you can't do that, then call me and I'll tell you just how beautiful you really are.

I will not be another flower,
picked for my beauty
and left to die.
I will be wild,
difficult to find,
and impossible to forget.

-Eric Van Vuren

Chapter 10
YOU ARE SMART

In this culture, if you don't make the honor role or the top ten percent, if you're not in an advanced math class or class for the more creative, or you don't get accepted to the smartest, most prestigious of colleges in the nation, you are deemed *not smart*.

This is so not true. You *are* smart, and never let anyone tell you otherwise. Being smart and wanting to utilize an education is attractive and empowering, so do it. Go for it.

I've never been in the top ten percent or been the smartest kid on the block. I can make terrific grades and do better than okay on standardized tests, above average, but I'm not a brainiac. I'm not a genius. I'm not someone whose brain can develop the software program of a computer.

Just do your best

When it comes to grades, my parents ask nothing of me. I push myself to the extremes: staying up till one or two in the morning on a normal school night, doing homework at every breathing moment, rewriting every single page of notes so that the information really sinks in. Yet, the work I did never seemed to cut it, never seemed to measure up to the number one student in my class.

Even if I put in all the work in the world, I still wouldn't be the smartest, and that took me a long time to come to terms with. But I at last realized one thing that would somewhat be the key to my life: just do your best.

As long as you're putting in the effort and exercising every single available resource into your work and your success, then that's all that matters. In essence, if you have the work ethic, the determination, the will to do great, then, I hate to break it to you, but you're smart.

If you have a brain, you are smart. If you are capable, you are smart. If you have an education, you are smart.

Think about it. Some people never even get the chance to experience the smartness that is right in front of you. Some babies are born without a brain and will never get the chance to live, to experience an education, to grow smart. Some children do not have access to an education due to family matters or geography. You do. You have access!

Not too long ago I read a book, *The Promise of a Pencil*, that changed my life in a number of ways. I didn't realize it until now, but I guess it did have an impact on my education. I've come to accept that having an education is a gift; going to school is a gift; having a pencil is a gift.

Use the gift of an education that is right in front of you. You are smart and capable. You already know this, I'm just here reiterating it. Use a pencil and do your best, and as long as you do those two things, you'll be fine. In fact, you'll be amazing.

I think the sexiest thing on anybody
is intelligence.
I respect someone who has a brain
and wants to use it
more than a pretty face and status.

-Sophia Bush

Chapter 11
THE UNKNOWN

Our lives are full of so many question marks. So many unsolved mysteries. Mysteries are the sweetest things in life; every single second you breathe, mysteries are happening all around you.

One word perfectly defines the meaning of the unknown: *serendipity*.

Serendipity means a series of events that happen by luck or by the unexpected chance, and they benefit a person in some magical way. I like to believe that the biggest, most monumental moments in our lives are serendipitous. How sweet it is to think that every happy, amazing, real moment happens by chance!

I also like to believe that your Creator, my Creator, has this plan where everything happens for a reason, but yet I still like to believe in the mysteries. These mysteries twist my mind; I'm often left feeling confused and conflicted, but that's what I believe is truly magical about the mysteries: our never truly knowing every single detail of life.

Life is rarely perfect. It seldom has been and almost never will be. Adding a bit of the unknown into the equation makes life even more enchanting, astonishing, and thrilling.

Mysteries compile this thing we get to live, life, and while the serendipity moments come to us, also the moments arise in time where the mystery leads us to question our beliefs, everything we stand for. Why is it that a little child dies of cancer? Why is it that some human decided to wake up one day and go blow up

> Don't be afraid of the unknown.

other humans, to kill them? Why is it that a person gets in their car and never returns home that day? Why is it that one person endures so much suffering when they do not deserve an ounce of misery?

These mysteries make me question what I believe: if I believe in serendipity, if I believe in my Creator, if I believe in fate. Yet, I think the essence of mysteries is that they always lead to something; maybe something that's bigger and better, maybe something that's smaller and worse; something that causes more suffering, or something that results in healing.

The mysteries that occur in our lifetimes make up who we are. They lead to the more substantial and brighter things in life, and they also lead to the things in our lives that cause pain. Yet, they all mold us into the people we were meant to be.

Don't be afraid of the unknown. Don't fear cancer, dying, pain, or suffering. Don't fear never knowing every single secret in this universe. Just live and understand that there is an unknown, that there is an ambiguous "X."

Accept the fact that the unknown molds us into the people we are meant to become, who we are destined to become. Embrace life at its fullest: the serendipity moments, the painful moments. Embrace all of it.

The expected is what keeps us steady.
It's the unexpected that
changes our lives forever.

-Meredith Grey

Chapter 12
MIND OVER MATTER

Every time I've felt discouraged, incapable, or pessimistic, my dad would always exclaim one of the most annoying phrases of all time: *mind over matter*.

Who knew that combination of words would one day become a mantra of my life?

Thank you, Dad, for often telling me I can do whatever I set my mind to. Because of you, I want to wake up and kick butt every single day. When I fall down, you better have no doubt in your mind that I'm going to get right back up.

Some physical things in life a human will never be able to accomplish: lifting a boulder, moving a skyscraper, propelling lightning from one's eyes—without a doubt, impossible. But mind over matter would disagree with that statement.

Mind over matter would say that, if you want to lift a boulder, then lift a damn boulder. Mind over matter would say that you can do absolutely anything. My dad would say that you can do absolutely anything.

The physical aspects are not the setbacks. Rather mentality is. You say you're not good enough to run a mile in four minutes, go run a mile in four minutes. You want to be the first female president of the United States of America, be the first female president of the United States of America. *Go after it!*

You are so much stronger than you give yourself credit for. Your body is so much more powerful than you perceive, but more than that, your mind is so much stronger than you believe.

An optimistic attitude is the key to mind over matter; a confident attitude is key to mind over matter. Tell yourself this every single day, "I can do it. I believe in myself. Mind over matter. I got this."

Mind over matter. It's simple.

> You are so much stronger than you give yourself credit for.

A strong woman
looks a challenge in the eye
and gives it a wink.

-Gina Carey

Chapter 13
THE MILES

As a runner, when I think of miles, benchmarks come to mind. I think of where I am and where I need to be. I reflect on the distance I've come and how far I still need to go. And that's life.

The miles indicate your growth as a person. Milestones through birthdays: at 16 you're deemed capable of operating a vehicle, at 18 you're deemed as an adult and fully grown up, at 21 you're deemed as allowed to be legally intoxicated, at 30 you're deemed old, at 40 you're deemed at about the midpoint of your life, at 50 you're deemed almost at the end, at 60 you're deemed really close to the end, and if you're lucky, then at 70 you're deemed at the end.

Look at all those years, all that life. The milestones do not have any right to deem you as anything because you're not. At 16, you're not ready to operate a vehicle because, let's face it, most drivers suck, and that goes for all drivers, even at the age of 60.

At 18, you're not fully grown up because none of us will ever be finished growing. Yes, our hormones at one point prevent us from growing further, but as souls, as characters, we never stop growing. The sun will never rise on the day we stop learning because learning is growing, growing is learning. We learn from each other, and therefore we grow. Birthday milestones mean nothing other than "Congratulations, you're an entire year older, you've made it another 365 days. Look at you go."

The miles mean we've come this far and have this more to go. The miles

> The miles
> are
> your life.

go by fast. They start off easy, with a bounce in your jog and not a bead of sweat on your face, and then they grow harder and harder, where you have nothing but beads of sweat streaming down your face. You become tired and restless, but the miles are what allow you to grow.

The miles are your life.

Embrace the miles and run each one like it was your last, and never ever stop growing. Don't let the miles fly by. Run them with a passion and a purpose. Time is truly of the essence.

It's the oldest story in the world.
One day you're seventeen and
planning for someday,
and then quietly, without you
ever really noticing,
someday is today,
and that someday is yesterday
and
this is your life.

-Nathan Scott

Chapter 14

IDENTITY'S MASK

Our society holds this preconceived idea that your success, your popularity, or your physical appearance defines who you are. *And that's so wrong.*

Identity is said to be found in religion, in love, in self-evaluation. And while I've always identified myself as a child of God, a person who loves a ton, and a person who is strong and determined, that's not my true identity. While those things—those labels—may be huge parts of my life, they're not who I am.

Often we're dubbed, labeled, and identified by our actions. If you do bad things, you're a bad person. If you do good things, you're a good person. *That's wrong.* I've had conversations with people who have been so disappointed and down in the dumps about themselves because of a grade they made or a poor choice they participated in. And I say one thing every time, "That does not define you."

And it's true. You are not defined and identified as a stupid person because you fail a test. That took me a long time to realize and come to terms with. I found it difficult to comprehend the idea of a bad grade not defining me. It was more of me listening to my own definition of myself instead of other people's definition of me.

But there's a difference.

When we identify who we are at our core, without the labels and opinions of other people, we seem to dig deeper into the identification; we care more. Because the worst thing we have to fear is disappointing ourselves: falling below standards, failing, not being good enough. When we listen to the opinions and identifications by other people, we seem to either take it all in or opt to not listen. And you never should.

Your true identity is how much you love and how much you are loved. The one thing people refer to about a specific person is always their identity. When we talk about someone who made a poor choice, we seem to refer to them solely as a bad person. That's wrong. Our legacies are our identities. If you loved a lot and were loved a lot, then that's your legacy and your identity.

We get so caught up in this idea, this concept, that identity is something we put on everyday. It's the makeup that we slather on our faces because we don't want to be recognized for what we believe we truly are.

Your identity is who you are at your core every second of every day of your entire life. And it's not a cover up, it's not a mask. Stop wearing a mask and pretending to be someone you're not.

Be bare. Be seen. Be identified.

To love and be loved, that's your true identity. That's your true definition.

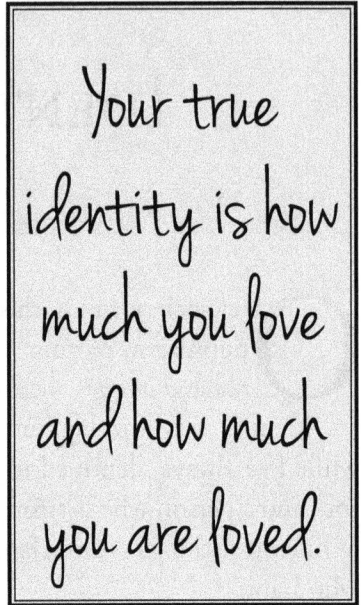

> Your true identity is how much you love and how much you are loved.

Your only identity is
'I am undefined and infinite.'
Any label you give yourself
limits yourself.

-Deepak Chopra

Chapter 15
WALKING IN CONFIDENCE

onfidence. An intimidating word.

Defined as a self-assurance that arises from your own appreciation of your own abilities and qualities, confidence is walking with your head up. Confidence is staying firm in your beliefs. Confidence is being you and being you in style, being you in your entirety and owning yourself.

We all struggle with it. It seems to come and go in waves, where one day you're so confident and proud of yourself and the body that you're in, and then the next you just want to remain inside of this bubble and avoid all social interaction for the fear of being put down. It's unhealthy. I know because I've been there. I was the kid who didn't interact for some time with almost anyone other than my family, for the fear of being made fun of, put down, or even judged. I was confined to my house because that's where I inserted myself, I made myself stick there like glue. I was unhappy because I was not confident.

It bothers me when people are uncomfortable in their own bodies. You were born in the body that you were blessed with. *Own it!*

> When you are confident, you are unstoppable.

But beyond body image, just be confident in yourself. You can do anything you set your mind to, so trust in yourself. Confidence, in short, is believing you can do anything, and trusting in your capabilities, in your wisdom, in your gifts.

When you are confident, you are unstoppable. No one or nothing can get in your way because you are firm in your beliefs, in your image, in your capabilities. A confident person is a person you want to be around and surround yourself with. Being in the presence of confident people should make you feel powerful and unstoppable. You should feel motivated to be confident, to rock everything you have.

I cannot chronicle how I got to be confident. Maybe it came from the combination of malignant people in my life, not knowing myself, not knowing my capabilities, and always having a constant fear of living, of life. Over time, I got rid of the malignancy, I made time to know myself, made an effort to know my capabilities, and became less afraid. I went outside of my comfort zone, and there I found people that I should surround myself with.

Once I found myself, I began to know myself and my capabilities. I ventured out and became more excited than scared. I looked at my life as a joyous ride full of adventures rather than a miserable ride full of fear. In self-discovery I found a passion, and in my passion I found my ultimate confidence.

Through the broadening of confidence, you become less and less associated with the fear of judgment. You care less of the opinions of others. You develop a sense of power in self. You believe you can conquer anything. You believe you are amazing. You believe in yourself.

Confidence is the key to happiness. Be confident in yourself because there's no one else in this world like you. There's only one you and you should be proud of that. Show your pride. Be proud of what you have and flaunt it. If you're confident, you have that right. Lead a confident life and a happy one at that.

Life is very short.
Insecurity is a waste of time.
-Diane Von Furstenberg

Chapter 16
THE SIMPLICITY OF LOVE

With so much hate and conflict and death and horror in this world, we find it easy to get sidetracked from the one thing that makes this earth go round: love. Saying three little words can change someone's life; love is what buys a stranger a cup of coffee; hugs transfer it to and from each other; we read love in sending an uplifting text.

Love is kindness.

Lately the topic of love vs. hate has been something my mind can't comprehend. I don't understand why a world can be full of so much hate. I fail to grasp why people are mean. I can't fathom why people decide to commit acts of hatred. The more and more I hear and think about these acts of hate, my heart breaks.

But what doesn't break my heart is love.

Love is powerful. Love conquers all. Love is invincible and inevitable. Love is the purest form of life.

So why do we find it so hard to love? Loving is not difficult. People just choose to not love and instead choose to hate.

Well, people, I choose to love. I decide to say three little words. I will buy a stranger a good ole cup of joe. I'll give someone a hug. I'll send an encouraging text. I'll practice kindness any day. All day, everyday I choose these things.

Love is not impossible. Every person is capable of expressing it to its fullest extent. It's right there. It's not far from you, right within your reach.

Love can change a person. Not the romantic love, rather I'm talking about the love of kindness. Not only is love giving, it's rewarding. Giving someone the experience of love through a cup of coffee or a hug spreads kindness.

Love is a movement. When you say three little words, you have spread a movement. When I give acts of love, acts of kindness, I am rewarded with the feelings of happiness, of hope, of warmth. My heart sings to the tune of love and of kindness. The heart beats on love. The world spins on love.

Love is scarce. Love is needed. Love is real.

Love is simple. Easy, giving, and rewarding. Love is easier than hate. Love is eternal, but hate is only temporary. Love conquers hate. Love mends broken hearts. Love cures diseases. Love gives a newfound meaning to life. To love is to live well.

Love is not impossible.

Spread love wherever you go.
Let no one ever come to you without
leaving happier.

-Mother Teresa

Chapter 17
FORGET ABOUT THE GUYS

Like every teenage girl, I have found myself wrapped up in the idea of guys, boyfriends, crushes, and feelings way too often. Four or five times too many, to be exact.

I've reassured myself that I'm confident and I don't need a guy to tell me how beautiful or how smart I am. And yet I have longed for some guy to say that. I see my closest of friends getting boyfriends and prom dates and I'm left feeling lonely and sad in the absence of a guy.

And it is so stupid! Guys are so not worth it, unless he's the right guy.

Finding validation in a guy—having someone tell you how beautiful you are, how smart you are, how important you are—is not necessary. You should never have to walk around feeling the teenage pressure to impress some guy. Do not sacrifice your sleep to text with some guy until dawn, when, the next thing you know, it was all for nothing because you've been friend-zoned.

My close friend has always told me that everything will happen in its time, as she always finds me longing for a boyfriend or some guy to come into my life and "sweep me off my feet."

Guys are not that important. There's so much more to your life than wasting precious time thinking about a guy. However, if you can't forget about the guys, then listen to the following.

I had a conversation with a friend one night, maybe not even a friend,

> The perfect girl doesn't exist.

just a person on the other end of the line, texting back, keeping me company. He asked me what I looked for in a guy, and my answer was someone who was genuine and kind, honest and real, hilarious and goofy, and most of all, someone who isn't afraid to be himself in the face of adversity and someone who is confident. That's what is really attractive, I told him, not the jaw-line of a guy or his six-pack, not the size of his biceps or the color of his hair.

No, physical appearances do not matter, at least not in my book. But it's as if every single guy wants a girl who meets every single physical characteristic of his dream girl. You know what? Screw them.

The perfect girl doesn't exist. There isn't a girl who is the total package. So many girls put so much time and effort into being this perfect girl who can meet the standards that a guy holds. Please stop. A guy should accept you, like you, and find you attractive just the way you are.

When I asked the guy on the phone what he looked for in a girl, he replied with physical characteristics, and I lost my shit. I told him he will never find a perfect girl and that he, like most guys, was wrong for only looking for physical characteristics in a girl.

He then went on to say something unnecessary and I went off on him, like this, word for word:

"1. No one knows what will happen in this life, so if I do or don't get married, then so be it. I'll live a good life either way.

2. If I'm meant to be a virgin my whole life or go without a kiss, then fine. If that means not being stuck with or in a relationship with a guy who is narrow minded, then so be it. I can live with the fact that I stayed firm in my beliefs and what I thought/think.

3. That comment really did frustrate me. Look, you're a cool person, but that comment may have made me think otherwise. It was just unnecessary and made me feel bad about myself.

4. I'm not naïve to the fact that most or all guys do only want a girl who meets every physical appearance of their fantasies. They'll just miss out on some really great souls who could do them some good in life. But I would

like to remain optimistic to the possibility that there could be some person out there who does not care about physical appearances.

5. I think I have a great ass and am smoking. So, you know what? (punching emoji)"

The point? Just be confident and know you do not need a guy to validate your beauty, worth, importance, or intelligence. Just 'do you' and know there is a plan, and maybe a guy is or isn't in that plan. The only guys who are worth it are the ones in your family and the ones who appreciate a girl for who she is on the inside.

And you,
you scare people because
you are whole
all by yourself.

-Lauren Alex Hopper

Chapter 18
THE PRESSURES OF LIFE

Perfection. Success. Status. Failure.

Clouds marked with those very words, those intimidating life or death words, hover over us like vultures. We're afraid we'll fail. We believe we have to be perfect. We believe we have to be successful. We believe we have to have an impressive status.

Those are the pressures of life.

You think about them almost everyday, and now more than ever for my high school friends. College is right around the corner. It's within reach. Your parents, your parents' friends, family members, all come up to you with two questions: where do you want to go to school and what do you want to study?

In other words, what are your plans, because you have no more than a few months to a year to figure them out...

And it seems like every choice of your life starts with what school you go to. It's scary. *I'm scared.*

There's a pressure to know what you're going to do with your life, and while that may not be the worst thing in the world to have figured out, it's also not the worst thing in the world not to have figured out. You're going to lead a wonderful life either way, regardless of which school you go to or which major you end up studying.

Failure is inevitable. Don't be afraid of it. It will come at some point in your life and it will kick you in the butt, knock you down, and maybe even make it hard to breathe. You'll get through it. What doesn't kill you makes you stronger, right, Kelly Clarkson?

It's as if every move we make has to be just perfect because, if not, then we fail, and our lives crumble from there. For the longest time I believed that. It made me sick, the idea we have to do every single little thing in life to a T.

I was so wrong. I learned that one of the best things in life is failure, because it doesn't kill you and it does make you stronger. What will kill you is caving into the pressure, into this idea that everything does have to be perfect. *Accept the failures.*

The reality is this: we are not perfect.

> Failure is inevitable. Don't be afraid of it.

We will not be successful for our entire lives. We will fail at one point or another. It's normal. It's something that may suck entirely, but in the end, you'll find your footing and be on your way again, wherever you're heading. Maybe that's a goal, or a place. You'll end up okay. Every little thing will be all right.

Just 'do you' and remember you are not perfect. You may not have the perfect success story. You may not have an impressive status. And yes, *you may fail.*

Embrace it. Live it. It's life.

*If at first you don't succeed...
you're normal!*

-Kid President

Chapter 19
THIS PURPOSE

When I think of the word 'purpose,' I believe I was put on this earth for a reason. And I so was.

What that purpose is, I have no clue. I wish I knew. A pretty good idea is dawning on me, bit by bit. I hope I'm right, but I'll do great things either way, and you should believe the same thing.

The Promise of a Pencil, you remember it, right? Written by Adam Braun, this book hands-down changed my life. That sounds so clichéd, that a book could change someone's life. It did, and gosh, I am so thankful for it.

Read it. Please, I beg you. It's about a man who's just trying to get through college and find his purpose in life. Through one journey and tons of adventures, he discovers it in the most unexpected part of the world at the most unexpected of times. He learns to breathe his purpose. He sees how to change the world.

And as I read the last word of the book, chills ran through my body. I felt empowered and motivated. I wanted to

> We learn from each other and in turn we grow off of each other.

go buy a one-way ticket to some unexpected place in the world and follow his same exact journey, but with my own unknown purpose.

Your purpose is probably unexpected. It's exciting and intriguing and scary at the same time, but the idea that you were put on this Earth for one reason and that's your purpose is so amazing. It's so almighty and powerful.

That idea just gives my body chills and I don't even think I can put into words what I'm feeling at this moment while considering my purpose; thinking about your purpose and about all of ours. You'll reach your purpose, regardless of which path you choose to follow.

It's all planned; it's all destiny; it's all fate. You'll get there one way or another. Just follow your heart and your calling.

In every interaction with someone, with another soul, we leave a little bit of ourselves behind. Maybe that's a memory, an idea, a scent, but we leave something behind. We learn from each other and in turn we grow off of each other. We're all one long connected vine that is feeding off of other people's ideas, love, comments, personalities. We're feeding off of each other's purposes, and it's extravagant.

You and I may not be the next Gandhi, the next Nelson Mandela, the next Mother Teresa, the next Martin Luther King Jr., the next Rosa Parks, or the next Adam Braun, but you and I, we're going to make something out of our purposes. It's going to be amazing and well worth the ride.

Your purpose is going to change lives. I know it.

Make your life a story worth telling.

-Adam Braun

Chapter 20

THEY SAY DREAMING IS FOR DREAMERS

Ever since I was a little girl, my dad always told me I can do whatever I want to do. Even if the idea was so farfetched, so out of this world, still I should go after it.

A dream of mine has always been to write a book. Such an accomplishment has always seemed so impossible, so farfetched. I've always believed that it's way too many words to put together and to try to navigate.

But I'm doing it. I've done it.

And that's not my only dream. I have many, many more.

When I was four or five and was asked what I wanted to be when I grew up, I always replied along the lines of a veterinarian. The typical answer for a kid was always either an athlete or a doctor, but no, not for me. I told you I was different, right?

Well, now I do indeed wish to become a doctor, so maybe I'm not so different. Our dreams change over time; heck, mine have changed numerous times. Yet, we still dream because what is a life without any dreaming? Dream on, my friends, dream!

It's similar to mind over matter. You must have the confidence in yourself that you can do anything you set your mind to. To dream is to have a passion. What sets your soul on fire. What makes you want to exert blood, sweat, and tears to achieve this goal, this life, this dream.

When I think of dreams, of dreamers, of dreaming, I think of the people who worked their butt off to get to where they are. People who came from nothing to something. I also think of *La La Land*, which is both weird and ironic, since I did not like that movie. We're all dreamers. We're all the people that came from nothing to something. We're all the Mia's and the Sebastian's who want to make it big, who want to be something.

You're a dreamer. I'm a dreamer. We're dreamers. Dreaming is what gives us a passion to live at the darkest of times. The notion that one day everything will be amazing because you'll be living your dream. There's absolutely nothing wrong with dreaming.

You want to do something so farfetched that it twists your brain a million different ways? *Do it. Go after it.* Go after your dream with everything you have.

Dream big. Dream the biggest of dreams. Dream the biggest of biggest of dreams. After all, you are a dreamer.

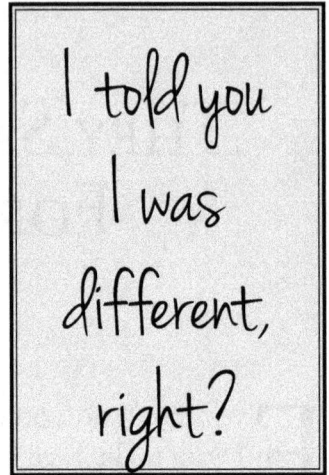

I told you I was different, right?

*They who dream by day
are cognizant of many things
which escape those who dream
only at night.*

-Edgar Allan Poe

Chapter 21

PUSHING THE LIMITS AND DEFYING THE ODDS

When life knocks you down, you have to get up. No excuses. *Get up.*

Yet, at times in our lives, we don't want to get up, because we feel like we can't go on. We would rather go into a fetal position and sleep and cry and complain because life is terrible.

But life is not terrible. At some point in your journey, odds are you will reach a breaking point. A point where there is no hope in sight. But odds also are that someone out there in this huge world has it much worse than you do. So no, life is not terrible. There is always some light and some glimmer of hope in an immense amount of darkness. Life is not as bad as you think. You can get through it. You're strong as hell, remember?

I cannot count the days where I just wanted to lie in bed and cry. I'm sure my parents didn't believe I could get through what I was enduring. They were always supportive, but deep down I suspect they had some major, frightening, intense doubts.

I defied their odds. I'm here today writing about defying odds. I did it! *Go, me!*

Being in a slump for a few years ends up digging a pretty deep hole that's hard to get out of. I didn't believe I could find my way out. I was always told that the light is at the end of the tunnel, it's so close, I'll see it one day. I never believed a word those people said.

It is so worth it.

Turns out they were right — thanks, everyone.

I found the light at the end of the tunnel, a tunnel that at first I had trouble believing I could navigate towards. My parents didn't imagine I'd be able to navigate towards it, and maybe even my friends agreed. I was in deep, but I got out. I pushed myself to the limits. It was hard and tiring, but man, was it worth it.

But for those of you who don't want to get out of bed, who don't want to live and experience and dream and succeed and be yourself, please do. It is so worth it.

When you're tired, when you want to sleep, when you want to quit, instead endure. Keep going. It may be hard and tiring. You may feel like the world is crumbling, like your life is crumbling into a million different pieces and you'll never be able to piece them together.

Your life is not over. Push through, you got this.

You can go on. Push your body to the limits. Let others believe you can't do something and go and do it anyway. Kick their thoughts in the butt. Go and get after it. Defy their odds.

You're stronger than you think, you really are.

Still, I rise.

-Maya Angelou

Chapter 22

JUST BREATHE

The easiest thing to explain in the world—yet the hardest to do—is the act of oxygen entering and leaving your lungs. Inspiration and expiration. Inhale and exhale. Easy to do at the easiest of times, but hard to do at the hardest of times. *Why?*

Life moves at such a rapid pace. One day, the world is spinning round and all is right, and the next, the world is spinning twice as fast and everything is just wrong. It feels like you can't breathe. As hard as you try to catch up, life moves faster than you, faster than you expected. It's hard to breathe because it's hard to find the time to actually inhale and exhale. You face deadlines, dates, appointments, places you need to be and people you need to see, people you need to take care of, but what about yourself? *You're forgetting you, aren't you?*

We so often forget to press the pause button, step back, and breathe. We forget to admit to ourselves that life is defeating us, we can't keep up, we can't catch up. It's okay not to be in control. Life isn't supposed to be. It's supposed to be chaotic and hard, but it's also supposed to be an amazing ride, and that's what makes it truly remarkable.

If there's one thing in this world I don't do enough of, it's breathing. Too often I forget to do it, and it only makes life that much harder. I'm a control freak: if I'm not driving the car, if I'm not navigating the plains, then life is out of control. I'll become anxious and stressed. I'll become someone who's not attractive to be around.

I forget to breathe.

> It's okay
> not to be
> in control.

I need to take more breaths. I need to take in this astounding life around me. I need to pause, take a step back, and take a breather. I have this bracelet that says 'breathe' in capital letters. I should wear it more, but I don't.

Here I am telling you to breathe and yet I can't do it myself. I'm a hypocrite. But that's okay. I'm learning to breathe, we all are.

Every once in a while, I hit the pause button. Give yourself that breather. The world may be spinning too fast, but you don't have to be. Navigate your own car at your own speed. Navigate the plains at how you see fit. You'll be okay in the end. Everything always turns out okay.

Breathe, my fellow grasshopper. Just breathe.

I've got to keep breathing.
It'll be my worst business mistake
if I don't.

-Steve Martin

Chapter 23

The Man Upstairs

Thus far, I've tried my hardest not to mention God. I have no idea why. Maybe because I wanted to remain open to other religions, or maybe because I wanted to dedicate a whole chapter to Him. Maybe even I've been trying to grow to my maximum potential spiritually. But everyday I'm growing in walking with Him.

All I can say at this moment is wow, *God is so amazing*. What a God we have!

I haven't had the "perfect" spiritual story. I've walked with Him for years, but never truly walked. I've claimed to be a believer; I've read verses; I've taped verses to my door; I've used verses as my screensaver, but I've never truly believed, until recently.

Not compared to that of an orphan or a homeless, hungry child, but I've endured a hard life, filled with my own personal pain and suffering, something I would never wish upon anyone.

Before starting this book, I never understood why I endured what I did, but now I do. Maybe it was to enable me to write this book, or maybe it was to appreciate life a little more, but whatever it was for, I understand it now. It all makes sense.

And while I may now have so much more knowledge about God and the bible and this walk of faith, I still have my doubts and questions. One thing I've been blessed with is friends willing and open to talking about God. Friends who will stay up with me until late in the morning and talk to me about God and the universe and the unknown. Friends who will send me verses I really needed to read that day. Friends who will write me notes that include a verse or two that I needed to hear.

In most of my conversations, the topics of our plans and the almightiness of the Lord always seem to come up. And now, more days than ever, I find myself understanding our plans and the power of God.

I held a recent conversation with a person I am so blessed to call one of my best friends. We talked about the beginning: how things started, how there was even a God in the first place, how our God could make a human body that was so intricately and perfectly designed.

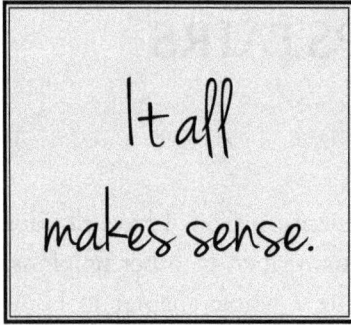

> It all makes sense.

That one, I have a hard time with, how our bodies are the way they are. Being an anatomy nerd, as you already read, I don't understand how our God could design such a complex body. A body where cells develop and multiply; a body where one organ pumps blood throughout an entire temple; a body where messages are sent and received. I don't understand it, it confuses me.

And in that conversation I said something like, "But faith is believing in the things we can't see and the things we can't physically touch." It's hard for me to comprehend, but the power of God is a faith that is so indestructible and powerful and almighty.

What I find the most amazing about God is that there are 7.4 billion-plus people on this planet, all made in His own image. And He loves every single person. He loves you regardless of anything wrong you may ever do.

He created us in His image for a purpose. He listens to every 7.4 billion plus people's prayers. He gives you your parents, your family, and your friends, He even allows you to have particular enemies. His timing is always spot on. He has a specific plan that connects every single person in some way.

That blows my mind. I'm astonished.

No perfect Christian exists, except Jesus himself. I have bibles, too many to count, that sit somewhere in my room and collect dust. I wish I would make more time to open them up and dive into His word.

I should. I will.

But that's the beauty of Christianity, I think. That there isn't a true, perfect Christian. That we all walk in our faith in our own way. That my walk in faith may not consist of opening up a bible every day or every week. That your walk in faith may consist of praying three times a day.

And the most amazing thing about God? He will walk with you in your own journey of faith, regardless of which path you choose. He listens to all prayers, He answers all prayers, He comes through no matter what.

What a glorious God that is! Man, are we blessed.

Not being able to fully understand God
is frustrating,
but it is ridiculous for us to think
we have the right to limit God to something
we are capable of comprehending.

-Francis Chan

Chapter 24

DANCE IT OUT, STAND IN THE SUN, AND BE YOUR OWN PERSON

If you know me, you know that I love *Grey's Anatomy*. If you don't know me, well, I hope you do now by reading this book, but hey, reader, I love *Grey's Anatomy*. The creator of that show, Shonda Rhimes, wrote a book, and this phrase, the title of this chapter, was on the cover: "Dance it out, stand in the sun, and be your own person."

Talk about an eye-opening moment.

Whenever I read it, happiness, authenticity, life, love, journeys, adventures fill my mind. Simply put, I think of life and every amazing thing that comes with it, the good, the bad, all of it, the whole package.

I'm going to dissect this quote piece by piece.

First, to dance it out means to live life to the fullest and embrace everything. To dance and be happy in times of adversity. To be an optimistic person with a positive attitude. To be free-spirited.

To stand in the sun means to be present in life. To experience the all so dreaded sunburns that turn into fabulous tans.

To be the one who dives into life when others don't, which leads us to being our own person. It means to be a leader instead of a follower. To create our own destiny. To be fearless in the pursuit of what sets our souls on fire. To march to the beat of our own drums.

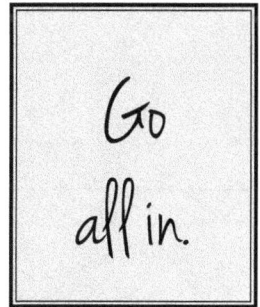

Go all in.

Put it together and you get to live life to the fullest. Go all in. Dance to the music you want to dance to, stand in the sun you want to stand in, and be the person you want to be.

I am different. I am an original.
And like everyone else,
I am here to take up space in the universe.
I do so with pride.

-Shonda Rhimes

Chapter 25

DEATH AT YOUR DOORSTEP

Death is inevitable. Yet, I'm still scared of it. We'll all meet it one day, but I find it alarming to fathom. But the worst thing to fear is fear itself, so let's dive in.

When most people consider death, it's a morbid topic. At lunch, my friends sometimes bring the topic up, and they often discuss ways they wish to die. They say they wish to go in their sleep or while drowning. It's all morbid, yet so true.

Death is something we shouldn't be afraid to talk about because we will all meet it one day. But when we do talk about death, the one thing we don't discuss is the legacy we want to leave behind. We never know what day we will be stripped from this earth. It could be today or tomorrow. It could be in twenty years or in seventy years. We have absolutely no clue.

But when that day does come, and death comes knocking at my doorstep, and I'm holding onto this planet with every fiber in me, I'll want to leave a lasting legacy behind. I want to change the world. I want to impact someone in some way. I want to do good.

So, when death and I do meet, I want to leave this earth with the legacy of changing lives, doing good, loving people, and being loved in return. I want to be remembered, not by my hair color or my personality, not by the money I made or the connections I had, but by the good I did.

That's what I want to be remembered by. That's what I want my legacy to be.

I used to have a quote on my door about death and when the time comes, how it will be easy to let go because of the life you will have fulfilled. It brought me comfort and hope. Comfort that the ones I leave behind will have felt my impact. Hope that I will do something extraordinary in this life.

I may be seventeen and young, and maybe even clueless, but what I am not is scared of death. When it knocks on my door at the time and day that God pleases it to be, I'll still go kicking and screaming, but I'll go leaving behind a legacy, and I hope to goodness it's a good one.

When I stand before God
at the end of my life,
I would hope that I would not have
a single bit of talent left,
and could say,
"I used everything you gave me."
-Erma Bombeck

Chapter 26

THE FINISH

It turns out that praying and wishing at 11:11 PM countess nights worked. I found happiness. I became strong, independent, fearless. I grew into a confident young woman. I became my own person.

I accepted myself for who I was, recognized the pain I endured, found the spark to fuel my happiness and keep me balanced. Before long, I figured out how to live life to the fullest, and I pictured life as a beautiful gift.

Then I flew with my own damn wings, while recognizing I was important through my immeasurable worth. Through my own validation, I realized I was beautiful and smart, not because of my grades, but because of the person I was becoming.

I accepted the unknown mysteries of life, so much that I adopted the phrase "mind over matter." I recognized that time is precious and not a label. Through love, I created my identity and learned to walk in confidence as I saw myself as a strong person.

As I recognized that love is the most powerful weapon in the world, I began to love. I told myself to forget about guys because they're not important, I said no to the pressures of life because I knew that failure was inevitable and perfection is unrealistic.

Through a book, I developed a sense of purpose. I learned to dream as big as I wanted because no one has the right to tell me I can't do something. By climbing out of a trench, I defied my own odds.

I learned I needed to breathe if I wanted to live another day. Because I became aware that God loved me, I grew in my faith.

I learned to dance it out and stand in the sun and be my own person because time is of the essence.

And lastly, I learned that I want to live a life worth telling.

I don't have it all figured out. I'm not perfect. I'm not old and wise. I'm young and ambitious. I want to live this life that we have been given. I want to do the impossible. I want to love. I want to fight. I want to do it all, and I hope that you do, too.

I want to live a life worth telling.

You ruin your life by desensitizing yourself.
We are all afraid to say too much, to feel too deeply,
to let people know what they mean to us.
Caring is not synonymous with crazy.
Expressing to someone how special they are to you
will make you vulnerable.
There is no denying that.
However, that is nothing to be ashamed of.
There is something breathtakingly beautiful
in the moments of smaller magic that occur
when you strip down and are honest
with those who are important to you.
Let that girl know she inspires you.
Tell your mother you love her
in front of your friends.
Express, express, express.
Open yourself up,
do not harden yourself to the world,
and be bold in who, and how, you love.
There is courage in that.

-Bianca Sparacino

•

ACKNOWLEDGEMENTS

Mom and Dad - Thank you for always being present. For being parents who not only provide for their kids, but love on and genuinely care for their kids. You two are my biggest cheerleaders, role-models, and hands down the best people I know. I love you two a whole lot.

Kennedy and Jaxon - You're my sibs and I love you two bunches. Thanks for always making me smile and laugh on the days when I needed it the most.

Nana and Papa Jon - Thanks for showing up to every game, birthday party, and holiday. For being involved in your grandkids' lives, I am eternally thankful. You two are the bomb diggity of grandparents.

Ang - I love you. Thanks for just talking to me and not only being a cousin but being a friend.

Smedian - I love you, girl, and I adore our friendship… It's the oldest one I've got! Thanks for always being there.

Arden, Kai, Rach, and Rhys - My friends. I love you girlies. Thanks for always being there for me as a shoulder to lean on, to cry on, and to laugh on… If that's even a thing. Your friendship, genuineness, kindness, and love is what has gotten me through these years, and for that, I am grateful.

Kendall Brooks - Thank you for being the teacher who not only teaches, but also cares about her students. Without you, I would not be where I am today. I love you!

Grace Mueller - Girl, you are awesome. Thank you for calling, texting, and reaching out when I needed a friend the most. Thank you for being my mentor and my friend, and more importantly, thank you for showing me the love of Christ. My walk with Jesus is all because of you.

Car and Add - Thanks for being there for me in the beginning. I miss and love you two so incredibly much.

Brooke Lewis - Thanks for being my friend, reading every single piece of writing, and just being you. You're a gift. Love you, bud.

I love you, fellow humans! I thank God everyday that you all are in my life. Man, I am one lucky gal.

ABOUT THE AUTHOR

Kaitlyn Harmon is a dreamer, believer, and aspiring adventurer. Born and partly raised in Southern California, she now lives in Austin, Texas, where she embarks on a new journey in life: college.

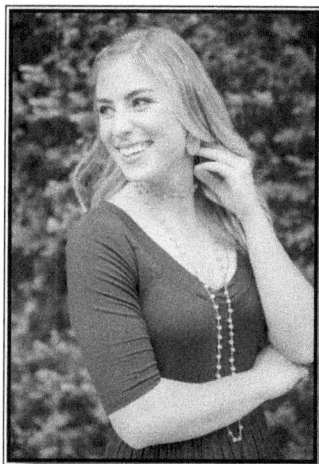

www.ingramcontent.com/pod-product-compliance
Lightning Source LLC
Chambersburg PA
CBHW060946040426
42445CB00011B/1027